CW00405401

OVER THE GARDEN WALL

Eden Press

OVER THE GARDEN WALL

Edited by
Rebecca Mee

First published in Great Britain in 2000 by Eden Press,
an imprint of
Penhaligon Page Ltd, Remus House, Coltsfoot Drive,
Woodston, Peterborough. PE2 9JX

© Copyright Contributors 1999

All rights reserved. No part of this publication may be
reproduced, stored in a retrieval system, or transmitted
in any form or by any means, without prior permission
from the author(s).

A Catalogue record for this book is available from the
British Library

ISBN 1 86226 574 7

Typesetting and layout, Penhaligon Page Ltd, England.
Printed and bound by Forward Press Ltd, England

Foreword

Over The Garden Wall is a compilation of poetry, featuring some of our finest poets. This book gives an insight into the essence of modern living and deals with the reality of life today. We think we have created an anthology with a universal appeal.

There are many technical aspects to the writing of poetry and Over The Garden Wall contains free verse and examples of more structured work from a wealth of talented poets.

Poetry is a coat of many colours. Today's poets write in a limitless array of styles: traditional rhyming poetry is as alive and kicking today as modern free verse. Language ranges from easily accessible to intricate and elusive.

Poems have a lot to offer in our fast-paced 'instant' world. Reading poems gives us an opportunity to sit back and explore ourselves and the world around us.

Contents

Garden Colour

My garden is a sight to see,
It is not perfect, one must agree,
But; it is my cup of tea.
Due to reasons unforeseen
I was banned from working there.

Two months have gone by
Without pulling a weed,
Strangely though, the plants are
Growing with great vigour indeed.

After the daffodils and the tulips,
Along came the paeonies
And the bright orange poppies,
Contrasting with the big yellow lilies.

Now the lavender hued perennial sweet peas are
Climbing in all their rampant glory through the shrubs,
Beautiful blue geraniums, nelly moser and soft pastel pink
Of the roses, the honeysuckle with rich scent,
The sweet williams too
And little doris bravely smiling through
The large white daisies,
Are all vying for attention.

The grass growing through, has turned to hay,
But by jove; they look more beautiful every day,
As they all intertwine
Having been left to their own devices.

Now as I come through the garden gate,
I may not see what I had hoped to see,
Yet, there is a hint of tranquillity filling the air,
The Kaleidoscope of colour is there, before me, in every hue.
What more could I ask for?

Mary Lawson

Our Garden

We moved to a flat
but it's lucky that
We have a garden back and front,
I still have a rockery,
rose bed and border,
And a small wildlife
pond made to order.
Husband's bonsai are
cosily placed on a shelf.
Attached to the shed
he made himself.
I sit in clematis corner
a patio surrounded by same.
I peruse all my plants
and make sure they all
have a name
Next year I may grow
tomatoes, but I don't think
there's room for potatoes.

Marjorie Calveley

I Spy In My Garden

This year there has been plenty of activity in our garden in one way or another; badgers eating hedgehogs, frogs leap frogging over each other round the garden, an army of snails covering our lawn after a storm, and a rescued baby house martin. But the most exciting event involved our bees.

We have always been pleased to see lots of bees circling our chimney stack for this would ensure plenty of pollination going on in the garden and an abundance of seeds and therefore flowers. One morning a deafening sound was heard. As we raced into the garden to look we saw bees everywhere. They were swarming. A short while later they had settled on our May tree and they now hung down in a cone-shape. Two days later they took off to go to the new home that the 'outriders' had found for them. We noted, however that there still seemed to be some bees left up on high coming and going as usual. A week later the same routine happened all over again only this time it was a smaller number of bees and they chose to hang from the apple tree. Our neighbours flocked to see both spectacles, and as if that was not enough excitement for one season, the other day a ferret put its head round the front door and came in for a look round. I was glad that he decided not to stay.

Alison Watkins

Gardener's Lament

I often think that all the odds
Are not stacked in our favour
When black and greenfly, slugs and snails
Are on their worst behaviour

Ladybirds that lurk indoors
Are not where they should be
For swarming up my roses
Is their breakfast, lunch and tea!

Squirrels excavate the bulbs
And bury nuts in borders
Pigeons pinch the ripening fruit
How many more marauders?

Where the seeds are newly planted
Sparrows scuff the earth to dust
The hollyhocks are looking seedy
Victims of the dreaded rust.

Wasps have sucked the juice from plums
My sunflower's just a dwarf
Now a thieving magpie's called
The fish have scarpered orfe!

Sheila J Leheup

4

My Father

'When I was a child I thought as a child' (Cor.13)

His Eternal self reclines upon the throne of grace.
Light glimmering down upon His crown
Through the motionless mist, His arms beckon with love.
Like a flowing river, peace cascades into my heart,
protecting me from all wounds.

'But when I became a man, I put away childish things'.

The journey is only just begun.
Learning to find peace and harmony with my Father.
The crossroads of life are altering my beliefs.
My cluttered thoughts obscure His face.
Which path will I take?
My Father will show me the way.

'He will be a lamp to my feet and a light to my path'. (Psalm 119)

And I will go in peace.

Stuart Cook

For Brenda

Though now for Brenda dear we mourn
We know we shall in time rejoice,
For she wakes to a brighter dawn:
Her time has come to be God's choice.

We know that one day we shall meet her,
When we from life to life ascend;
And with what joy shall we then greet her.
As daughter, mother, wife and friend.

Eric W Baker

God's Gifts Of Nature

Gazed outside and watched the darkening clouds,
The sun appeared and I cried out aloud.
God's gifts of nature cost nothing to enjoy,
Some take time and all our senses employ.
Best of all, watch the stars out at night,
For what could better this amazing sight.

S Mullinger

I'm Not The One To Convert

You don't have to go to church,
to be a Christian.
I heard a lady say.
I don't need a wooden pew,
to get on my knees and pray.

But you don't get the feelings and wonder,
though I'm not the one to convert.
You're missing the sights and pleasures,
I get by going to church.

You don't see the man in our choir,
Blind, yet singing from his book of braille.
Or our 99 year old veteran, struggling
to reach the communion rail.

You won't hear of Anne and Ron,
Missionaries in China on our behalf.
Or the cat walking up to the altar,
making the whole church laugh.

No, you don't have to go to church,
to be a Christian.
Stay at home, bake a cake, watch TV
But you won't get your heart uplifted,
And walk home smiling, feeling grateful,
Yet somehow free.

Sue Knott

Church Building

Emmanuel, like an upturned ark
yawning at the sky
through the demolition,
was reduced to bare boards
and bricks, no choir song.
Autumn shuffled round its
slow sinking into neat
piles of salvage.

But in Saint James,
a large congregation
watched the Bishop,
in a flash of fiery
cloak, as he led
nine newly-confirmed
adults through the
church to the narthex.

There the new Emmanuel stood
accessible (blueprints, model on table)
and the people smiled, congratulated
these emotional new Christians.
They drank tea, sold
tickets for fund-raisers
became part of the body of the church.
Breathed in the moment.

The lady whose daughter was
Emmanuel's last bride,
knows that a grandchild
is on the way.
She prays that the new
Emmanuel will be built
in time for the child
to have the first baptism there.

Lee Turley

Jehovah Jireh - My Provider

I meet you in your struggles
And can show you how to live.
I'm standing there beside you
To encourage and forgive.
Come to Me in all your pain,
Those feelings that destroy.
Feed on Me, the bread of life
And sorrow turns to joy.
I may not take away the hurdles
But will give you strength to jump;
And for the pain
Pour in the oil
That fills the emptiness -
Overflowing soothing balm
Ministers My grace.

Those things that seemed impossible
Now have a special place.

Hilary A Brinkman

Test Of Faith
(To Noel)

And they said: 'What does your faith say
to the cancer sufferer?
How do you believe in God
in the face of the world's pain?'
They shook my faith in their teeth
like a dog shakes an old slipper.

And I said: 'It is not for me to know the ways of God.
He is too great for me to package
in a mouthful you can swallow,
but I believe that in our living
and our dying there is meaning.'

And they said: 'What good is that to us?
What will you do when we are dying?
What will you say to us then?'

'There is nothing I can say,' I said,
'But I will love you.
I will be there until the end
and I will hold your hand
and soothe your fevered brow.
And I will commend you into the care
of the eternal God.
And at your passing from me,
I shall weep and smile at once
for I shall know that He has heard
my prayer, and will do most sumptuously
for you what I could only
most imperfectly attempt.'

At this they smiled and put the slipper down.
In the tenderness, not in the explanations,
there is God. Even in the pain.

Pippa Thorneycroft

A Winter's Tale

Summer, are you now but a distant spirit
Where God's *creation, was, within it*
Are you but a distant ghost
Where laid the beauty of the gentle *Host.*

Autumn are you now, but a distant shade
Where the green bracken turned bronze
                                    from the glade
Where once the shadows were - bright and burning
When trees were still covered, and yet whispering

Winter are you, - but a servant
Where *God's Beauty Was Then Present*
When flowers were blossoming in the sun
But, now you are here to overcome

Now, winter months are drawing nigh
Why, cover the beauty of the sky
Where owls just perch, and stand, and stare
Till, the mist covers the damp night air

Oh, winter, are you the keeper of the cold
The frost that shimmers so very bold
While, icicles, settle on the windowpane
And the icy snow is settled once again

Spring come again quickly to bring us warm days
When sunbeams peep through, in so many ways
When blackbirds are back, with songs of rejoice
While the thrush joins in, with their tender voice

When the chaffinch sings, with the song of the swallow
Such a chorus starts, as they perch on an orchard bough
Building their nests, till early twilight
Till, nightingales are heard, under the starry height

When the four winds blow, through the autumn and winter
Till, the winter ceases, and the spring meets the summer.

Jean P McGovern

The Symphony Of Life

As we play the ongoing symphony of life,
We find some notes are shrill and full of
                                        strife,
While some cascade in light and happy flow,
When days are rich with joy and brightly
                                        glow.
At times there is a long and silent rest
Enabling us to pause and listen, lest
We forget the heavenly music, which around
Us plays with pure melodious sound,
In perfect harmony with no discordant note,
Reminding us the great Conductor is not remote,
But waves His baton with arms of love,
So that our Symphonies may join with those
                                        above.

Brenda Tate

It Came Upon A Midnight Clear

Come join with us to celebrate
The birthday of your King.
A wondrous joy bestowed on us
So, let's rejoice and sing.
The angels brought the tiny babe
To save our souls from sin.
The stars were bright that glorious night
When Mary welcomed Him.

The shepherds gave a simple lamb,
Their humble gift of love.
They knelt to pray in deep respect
While God looked from above.
His precious Son He'd given us
Explaining right from wrong;
So raise your voices loud and clear,
Triumphant in your song.

And now two thousand years have passed
Since Jesus came to stay.
He showed us hope and peace and love
And how to spend each day.
So let's respond devotedly,
In worship, prayer and voice,
Rememb'ring God's eternal wish,
Sing our praises and rejoice.

Gwenda Bleasdale

Christian Messengers

The love of God is all around, I know some don't believe it.
I wasn't sure myself at first I thought it was all lies.
Then one day when disaster struck I needed someone near.
My friends were all too busy to lend a loving ear.
So I sat down and tried to ask for someone to show a way,
that all this heavy burden could be taken far away.
It was on a Sunday morning I walked into the Church,
and sat right at the back not wanting to disturb.
And when the service was over two people came to me . . .
then three and four and several more,
all shaking hands and greeting me.
I suddenly found I had more friends
than I thought could ever be.
They showed me God had time to spare
and showed me how to ask in prayer.
I asked Him and He told me that He loved me very much.
And now when I am in despair,
I talk with my friends to God in prayer.

Ann Boffey

The Gardener

Now closer to God than any man
I tread softly now to see if I can
Imagine his dreams, his plans, his thoughts
Of tulips, roses, forget-me-nots.

Mother Nature knows him well
He's one of her helpers, and she could tell
Of his capable hands, his caring ways
Of nursing his flowers through sunlit days

He lifts a bulb, holds it up
Tenderly as a loving cup
What are his thoughts? this quiet man
Are they of his family and how it began?

His garden is a joy to see
A riot of colours, where every bee
Can drink its fill from dusk till dawn
And fly off happy - its life goes on.

Now he turns over the earth
To give his seeds and bulbs rebirth
He coaxes, cajoles and gently handles
With a light on his face from a hundred candles

His old bulbs he's safely tucked away
To grow and bring pleasure another day
To people who pass by his place
Some of them stand and longingly gaze
At the creation of this gentle man
Who, surely is part of God's great plan
To spread peace and joy with his garden of flowers
To heal a sore heart in its darkest hours

All this time not a word have I spoken
He greets me now, the spell is broken.

Christina H Mackay

Your Love Shared

Sharing your love Lord, between us
gives us new hope every day.
Whatever our need is, you know it
and someone is told how to care.

Sharing your love between us,
shows how you want us to be.
To help mould our lives, through your spirit.
To learn of the truths you reveal.

Sharing your love between us,
building a kingdom for you.
Bringing you glory and honour,
as others look to you too.

Sharing your love between us,
strengthens promises you have made.
Answers to prayer means a blessing
as we seek to ask and receive.

Thank you for the gift of love Lord,
as we meet together as one.
Thank you that we are united,
through your greatest love as the Son.

Mary M Dorey

Millennium

With January, a jamboree of unimagined fun
Sees the folks fling up their hats - two thousand years (and one).
Around the dome at Greenwich, up and down the motorway,
They bang their drums, string up the lights
To celebrate their day.

And tossing to the whirling winds all semblance of concern
They have a feast, let crackers off, watch bills and taxes burn!
The cheers ring out how honouring their ideal, Superman,
The message sweeps around the world -
'Just look what he has done!'

But sighing through the Stock Exchange and halls of Parliament
Another sound, a hint of fear, unnerved and hesitant,
Finds crawling from the woodwork of the nation's centre stage
Computer bugs, 'fifth columnists',
The stuff of sabotage!

So might the bright bonanza, the millennium's festival,
Shout promises, declare itself an timeless spectacle -
There's nothing quite so simple in the world that man has made.
His dark desires, explosive powers,
Somewhere the traps have laid.

And when he thinks he rules the earth, his pride becomes a joke!
Those tough Atlantic e-mails and that Middle-Eastern cloak
Of 'holy' resolutions drown the crying of the young -
His noisy bluster only hides
The ruin he will bring.

He needs a kick to wake him up to what the 'new world' is -
Not January's 'house of cards' but God's own palaces.
And where his cosy visions meet a sudden, awful chop
He needs to see God stand beyond
Alone and lifted up.

Priscilla Judd

18

Undeniable Love

When I cried, You held my hand
No questions asked or solutions planned
You simply listened and simply loved
Protecting me from the darkness above.
Placing trust in unknown ground
Knowing not what may be found
Just being there was what You gave
Reaching out, my life to save
My tears You dried, I know not why
You could have left my soul to die
Instead You touched me deep inside
Showed me You were at my side
Never to leave or hurt me more
Friendship with an open door.
You gave me a gift of so much worth
That's seldom found upon the earth
The gift of life You freely gave
To break my heartache, and live the life I craved!

Kirsty Donald

The Lily And The Lamb

Can anyone really know or care. Can anyone cast away his
                                                    doubts?
Can anyone pause and say to me 'There is no God about' -

He's there with me above the trees - Beneath the surging foam
In sweetest birdsong - In the night. In dusky scented woods.
In cuckoo call and first day light - in good times and in bad
In pain, despair and anguish deep, His love surrounds and cares.

Can anyone watch his vigilance? Can anyone say to me. There are
other Gods. My faith is here within my heart
A fluttering beautiful bird
His feathers are as bright as day and strong to soar above!
The angels wait. The Lamb grows strong. The lily's perfume wafts
along the stranded shore of life, to meet with me above.
Then perfect rest within his arms.
'The Lily and the Lamb' - The pangs of death no more to feel.
My Lily and *my* Lamb.

Carol Palmer-Ayres

Help!

Lord, I'm tired.
I'm tired of feeling empty inside
of smiling on the outside
while inside I'm crying.
I'm tired of being *constantly* in pain
of being restricted
in a body that only half works.
I'm tired of being different,
of standing out in the crowd,
of fighting (even 'the good fight').
Lord, You know how I long to be loved.
I'm tired and I need Your healing
of the mental pain
of the physical pain.
I need You to fill me anew,
to show me *Your* love.

G M Archer

Cabbages

Q   What part of a cabbage can't you eat?
A   His wheelchair.

Cabbages are green, inanimate, with curly leaves.
Ever seen a green man?
Ever seen a man sprout leaves?

Cabbages are edible, full of vitamins;
Go down well with roast beef and Yorkshire pudding.
When was the last time you ate boiled man with your dinner?

Man can see, hear, feel;
Would you be seen talking to a cabbage,
Or giving one a cuddle?

Man sings, laughs, cries, makes noises;
When did you hear a cabbage laugh?
Or shout in sheer frustration at something it couldn't do?

Man has individual tastes;
Ever calmed down a frustrated cabbage with soothing music,
Or tried to feed it with food it didn't like?

How often do you see people pushing cabbages in wheelchairs?
And tell me, -
Where does it say 'God made cabbage in his own image'?

Kathy Rawstron

Trees On A Windy Day In February

Evergreen ostrich feather fans
Swaying in some eastern palace,
Bowing low to appease the pride
Of satin turbaned potentates.

Deciduous trees naked and bare,
Sickly branches with slender twigs
Reaching heavenwards like starving children,
Skinny hands pleading for bread.

Richest green and grey most drab,
Supreme joy and deepest pain,
Side by side in a world
Which groans for its Creator.

Janet Sewter

Redemption

My God, my God, why have you forsaken me?
The cry rings out from a Saviour on the cross.
You knew the depths of pain and suffering,
That even God had turned his eyes from sin.

Out there, in a world torn and frustrated,
That cry goes up from hearts in pain.
Can there be no forgiveness, no beginning
Of hope and an end to suffering?

That cry is in my heart, an echo
Of the world's great, dark despair.
I *know* that God forgives and turns again
To see the lost who call in pain to him.

But how, Oh Lord, can this great multitude
Of suffering souls be reached for you,
Without a church, without some others
To bring them hope and show your love?

Lesley Blythe

A Troubled World

Today we live with terror, murder, fearful deeds,
That darken all our earth,
And sown within our children's hearts are
hatred's seeds,
To give a bitter birth.

To live in freedom man must never lose his right,
Despite the awful cost,
And, as through years past, for this he still
must fight,
Or else his soul is lost.

But men have lived since dawn of time with wars
and fears,
And, as in Spring again,
From winter's sombre death rebirth of life appears
So one day peace must reign.

Ruth M Shallard

On Golgotha

Darkness lies heavy on Golgotha hill,
Darkness at noon;
Three wooden crosses on Golgotha hill -
Death coming soon.

Crowds come to mock him on Golgotha hill,
Friends grieve below;
Death is approaching on Golgotha hill -
Death coming slow.

Jesus cries out upon Golgotha hill,
Last dying breath;
Jesus is silent on Golgotha hill -
Silent as death.

Peter English

Bread

(See John's Gospel, chapter 6)

Fresh and fragrant,
     Wholesome food,
Crusty, crumbly,
     Chewy, good,
Proved and risen,
     Making us grow
Strong and Healthy,
     Goodness to know,
Goodness to share.
     Satisfying and sustaining,
Energy and life maintaining,
     Daily portion,
Warmth and healing,
     Digestible and
Sense-appealing,
     'I am the Bread of Life',
Said the Lord --
     Jesus, come, live in me.
Teach me your Word.
     Satisfy my hunger, deep within,
Strengthen me and heal my pain.
     I shall never be hungry again.

Vivien Wilkinson

Remembrance Sunday

The profit of their ceremonial gift
The English manifest most achingly
Though acts of mourning, songs in minor key,
Is thought that wrenches, makes the heart uplift
Beyond the daily things that melt and shift,
Into a stillness, as the town falls still,
Into a silence neither strained nor ill
But kind and melancholy, like the leaves that drift
In sombre sweetness through the pensive air.
The robes and medals, drums and harmony,
The flags and trumpets, swords and heraldry
No bitterness or triumph can declare
But wholesome silence, decorous and spare.
Grieving and glad, a voiceless psalmody.

Trevor Humphreys

Tapestry

The weaver wove a tapestry of colours, bright and pale,
and with each thread
she told a tale:

Blue the mantle o'er the maiden's head
as she kneads the dough
to bake the bread.

Pure white the feathers of the angel's wings
as he whispers low
the message he brings.

Golden the smile on the carpenter's face
enfolding the maiden
in a loving embrace.

Grey the fur of the donkey so strong
as he carries the maiden
on the journey so long.

Dark as ink the night, silver the moon
as she birthed her baby
in a stable room.

Scarlet the threads for the babe from above
the colour of blood,
the colour of Love.

Jo O'Farrell

He Came To Us

O yes He came to us,
God's only Son.
He lived this life with us,
The anointed one.
For many years the prophets had foretold
A saviour King would come.
He healed the sick, and caught
Attention when He taught
The testament He brought
For all mankind to hear.

O yes He tried for us,
For me for you,
Was crucified for us,
For me for you.
The air was rent with the cry
'Forgive them Lord for they
know not what they do.'
He'd been denied by us,
The wicked and the just,
And still He died for us
According to the word.

The Spirit's with us here
In all we do,
And when we shed a tear
It sees us through.
With all the troubles and temptations
That surround us everywhere,
It keeps the purpose clear
In all we ought to fear
When sinfulness is near
It keeps us all from harm.

Gill and Michael Whitten

Family Traditions

Dwell together in families is the message
given us by the good book
the home in which families can dwell
can be a haven of peace
or a prison of turmoil
for most children experiencing either
back to basics for most families
means being more tolerant towards each other
this pattern for most lasts longer this century
perhaps too much to ask of human beings
travelling the road of life
with foremost a family to love
share troubles and bring children up
to respect the message of
dwell together in families this
being the safest haven from
a troubled world around us.

Janet Glew

Untitled

One man gave an empty stable
it is all I have said he.
Another gave his life
that ours might not empty be
He came to us, by lowly birth
to tell the people here on earth
that *He* the Lord of all creation
had come to them with salvation
and for those who believed in him
from them he took away their sin
as we look upon that man and ponder
on his life of grace and wonder
He really did walk upon the sea
and many were healed around Galilee
and then, for you and me he died
but sent the holy spirit to be inside
of those who want to know
the truth, the life, the way to go.

Fred Tobin

Christian Thoughts On The New Millennium
To Those Who Went Before

When the bells ring out on New Year's Eve.
A new century will be born.
They will be joyfully telling all,
To make the most of this happy morn.

Not everyone meets a new century,
For they only happen every hundred years, you see.
But those who do should thank their guiding star,
And stop to think how lucky they are.

Each new year brings its own jollification,
But heralding in a new century calls for special celebration.
Why not think of the many who have passed this way
And helped bring us to this momentous day?

Let's hope that the new century will give,
Added fervour to all that live.
But may all conflicts of the past,
Be mindful to the very last.

I've heard it said that those years are best forgotten,
As everything in them was rotten.
But think again where would we be today,
If folk had not fought hard, in their own way?

Everyone learnt the basic laws of giving,
And found true happiness in living.
No-one stopped to count the cost,
For if they did we'd sure be lost.

Betty Green

The Twenty-First Century

Have we not learned in 2000 years
the lesson our Saviour has taught,
to live in peace with our fellowmen
not to fight, for life is so short.

After 2000 years can we not find a way
to live by the rules he has set,
it shouldn't be hard to love one-another
but sadly we haven't learnt yet.

Edna Cosby

The Millennium

Christ's love has spanned two thousand years,
In peace and war, in the good times and the bad.
His love by sacrifice was sealed
And burgeoned all through man's hopes and fears
In all the nations' toil, in the good years and the sad,
In the crises of men's lives, in sudden stress concealed.
In the evening of our days, in peaceful joy revealed.

Christ's love is shown in gifts of grace,
In direst war, in the longed-for end of strife,
In our times of prayer and in our doubts and fears.
In agony and joy, may we see His face
Serene above the mists of life
And hear His word that echoes down the years.

In happiness and in bitter days distraught,
We thank our God for all that He has brought
Within our lives, for the laughter and the tears,
For all our days of calm and all, our peace at night.
We thank our God for all that He has taught
Through all the movement of the years
For all His love and for His gift of light and light.

Uvedale Tristram

A Moment In Time

Two thousand years!
Not one!
A brief moment in the eons since creation:
When first God raised the land,
Spread wide the seas
And set His lights
In the dark heavens.

Strange creatures flew
And crawled and swam
As man first walked the land
And with his help-mate
Peopled the earth with human progeny.

A human race that was to stray
Far from God's loving plans for it.
Until -
Until that moment
We remember now
When God to us
Gave His most precious gift -
Jesus, His Son!

God became man two thousand years ago.
He lived upon this earth too short a time,
This Son of God.
Cut off by cruel death,
Condemned by those He came to save.

And we, at this Millennium,
Look back:
Not on one thousand years,
But two!
Back to a humble stable in a far off land;
And know that our God's love for all mankind
Transcends all earthly love.

He gave his only Son
To live and die for us,
Yet still we turn our backs on such great love.
Still, in this world of wars and strife,
God's teaching -
'Love thy neighbour' -
Is but a faint and distant voice
Amid the tumult of our Godless lives.

Roma Davies

Birth

Ship sinking away,
Into black all night space,
Weightless, away through galaxies,
Sailing one wind way,
Twinkling lights around,
Above, below, left, right.
Aeons dead old and alive.

Young on distance travelled,
Old as history reborn,
Warmth arrive on course,
Brightly lit solar system.

Sphere of breath
Life eternally, externally,
Lit.

Derek Robert Hayes

A New Beginning

A new century and a new beginning,
another chance to live a better life.
Perhaps with a more Christian attitude
than one has previously shown, this we
may only admit to one's self, alone.

The year 2000 looms excitingly near
And in our hearts we lovingly acknowledge
the most celebrated birth.
Baby, Jesus, born to bring peace, hope and
love, to all generations, on earth.
Only are we Christians, if we think and act,
with understanding and care.
Wanting better standards and conditions for the
elderly through effort and prayer.
Thoughts for the many people that are on the bread
line, their life is hard and unsure.
Oh! for them to have a more meaningful life in the
immediate future.
Life styles have changed drastically since Jesus
walked the earth.
But human nature remains the same, and many are
searching for their heaven on earth.
If only dear Father God, the end of hunger, fear and
crime was in sight.
And everyone had a roof over their head, never to be
forced from their homes in the middle of the night.
If only in the Millennium everyone could keep their dignity,
and walk tall and proud, what a wonderful world it would be.
We need peace, and love in the Millennium for all nations to
unite in harmony.

Elizabeth Myra Crellin

Love In Time

Look to the eyes of the stranger in Bethlehem;
see in them God before time began.
Innocent babe of an innocent mother; the
child is an innocent as a lamb -
come to purge our sinfulness;
yet to offer hopefulness.
'Love' comes down in time for all of us.
As was ever, now and shall be.
Look to the stranger in Bethlehem!

Look to the eyes of a young boy in Nazareth
learning his trade as his work began;
growing to know that a destiny calls to him;
loving, obedient, tall young man.
Mary watch your son mature;
Joseph help him be secure.
'Love' come down in time for all of us.
As was ever, now and shall be.
Look to the young man of Nazareth!

Look to the eyes of the stranger in Galilee
gathering helpers, his time begun;
calling to all 'Be disciples and follow me
and I will teach you as 'God the Son'.'
As they journeyed on their way,
some would listen, some would say -
'This is 'Love' come down for all of us.'
As was ever, now and shall be.
Look to the stranger in Galilee!

Look to the eyes of the stranger on Calvary;
see in them 'Love' before time began.
Innocent Son of an innocent Mother, he
offers his sacrifice like a Lamb.
Burdened man, how can this be?
Are you purging sin for me?
'Love' hangs there in time for all of us!
As was ever, now and shall be.
Look to the stranger on Calvary!

Look to the eyes of the stranger whose jubilee
fell upon us as our time began;
who by his birth and his manhood and ministry
calls upon us as our 'God made man'.
Know his life was spent for us;
Saviour, risen glorious!
'Love' is here in time for all of us.
Bethlehem! Nazareth! Galilee! Calvary!
Stranger no more as we shout for joy!
As was ever, now and shall be.
'Love' is the time of our Jubilee!

A Hemson

Ring Out The Bells!

Two thousand years of faith and doubt and strife -
We celebrate the perfect human life:
>> Not humanity alone
>> But God-made-Man.

Two thousand years is but a drop
In the ocean of time.
For those sad folk who know not God
Why celebrate at all
With crackers and streamers and an unwanted dome,
Street parties in winter to which few will come?

Why do we celebrate this special time and date
If not to praise and honour Him for whom we wait?
>> Without this thought
>> It all means naught.

Ring out the bells to celebrate
>> The Jubilee of Christ!

E D Sulston

The New Millennium

What joy to think we have been invited to express our thoughts in
Poetry for Today.
It is a golden opportunity to put our thoughts into reality as we think
of this great subject.
As we are nearing this special year we think of Christ born two
thousand years ago.
As he grew older he started to preach the gospel.
Now a great part of the world knows about him, maybe many will
find Him through this special year as there own Saviour.
After the good work he had done they crucified Him.
Yet the good Lord forgive them they know not what they do.
What a lesson for us all to learn.
Almighty God creator of mankind gave us a world with all its riches.
He is always with us when we have a problem we go to Him.
Most of the world is taking part in the Millennium.
I wonder what we can do.
We hold the key, let us turn the lock, saying this is our finest year.

Thomas Hancock

An Allergy In A Planetary Graveyard

The curfew tolls the knell
Of parting age
Thank God -
My nervous-system seeks
A calmer stage
For
To those who look
It is very plain to see
That I suffer from
A Twenty-first Century allergy.

I cannot tolerate the modern
Strain and stress
The motorways, the videos
The mobile phones . . .
But nonetheless
I struggle on and on and on
Ungraciously
For I am suffering from
A Twenty-first-Century allergy.

Some people take to the world
As duck to water
But I am like a lamb
Led to the slaughter
I toil, I strain
And carry on relentlessly
But I am suffering from
A Twenty-first-Century allergy.

The New Millennium has knocked upon the door
I am open to its presence
More and more
Although some cling to the present
It's just not my cup of tea
For I am suffering from
A Twenty-first-Century allergy.

J C Crowe

Rays Of Blight

I opened my weary eyes
At the first glimpse of light
Sad and bad about today,
This day - another long day
Marking, yet a new epic,
Of another thousand years
In the vicious cycle of life.

I wish this day were tomorrow
And Oh! How fervently I wish
That tomorrow'd never come
But our 'tomorrow' is now here
Cast in the mould of yesterday
A portent of an expiring hope.

I have seen people dying,
Broken on the eve of a new era
Not in body but in hopelessness;
Many who'd laid their faith in fate
Looking ahead to a fulfilling life
On the other side of the epic,
But such dream totally had faded.

I could see far into the distance
To the dawn of a new life source,
That place many had tried to avoid
But are now trudging inextricably to,
I feel my being drawn to this spot
Sucked up in the vortex of time,
And my will too weakened to duel.

I wish I could retrace my steps
Back to the childhood of the ages
That side of life's thousand years
When all things were beautiful
- A paradise of infant joy -
Where man was given to live
To the brim many years of bliss.

Alexander Adegbile

Millennium

Moments of joy, moments of sorrow
Indelibly engraven in our story,
Leading onwards to the morrow,
Looking back over past glory.
Endings, beginnings, merge,
Nudging us forward in a continuum
Nights and days surge
Into the new Millennium,
Unfurling two thousand years of
                            Christianity.
Mystery of God in humanity.

Sister St Joseph

Christian Thoughts For The Millennium

Christ, Master Of History
BC and AD refer to milestones
Indeed Jesus Christ's birth and death mean cornerstones
His Church remains a rock when storms shake the Holy See,
On the waves of life, the Pope acts like a captain at sea.

The Cross
Who will ever praise its presence?
Who can say so much in silence?
Who will build such a world unity?
Who cam raise such a stream of charity?

The Bible, A Best-seller
The Book is revered through the centuries,
Read even when forbidden in some countries,
This sacred Book links people and feed their belief,
It sparks dialogue and spiritual relief.

Rome, The Eternal City
The real hub where all the roads are leading,
The City where the Church's heart is beating,
There we near the cradle of civilisation,
There lives the Pope who wins our admiration.

Fame And Name Of The RCC
Blessed are the founders of churchtowers
And those who honour Christ, like painters, writers.
Blessed are the monks, their abbeys, real hives,
And the nuns and nurses who devote their lives.
Blessed are all those faithful Christians
And all the Good Samaritans.

All of them open the gate of the new century,
Whatever their race or native country.

Paul Jean

Christian Thoughts

Rather than think - what a life
be thankful to God you have a life
Rather than think - this garden's a chore
be thankful to God there's so much more

Rather than think - who's scratched my car
be thankful to God - you're who you are
Rather than think - children cause worry
be thankful to God - they're all healthy

Rather than think - this house is too big
be thankful to God - you've somewhere to live
Rather than think - the pain in my back
be thankful to God - you're still intact

Rather than think - what's life all about
be thankful to God - you're in with a shout
Rather than think - why can't I sleep
be thankful to God - as there's many who weep

Don't be misled I've had all these thoughts
brought to my knees - I almost baulk
So much tragedy around the world
some people don't have any will to talk

Rather than think- doesn't anyone care
be thankful to God - that he is there
It's pure survival for all the poor
I pray for them daily that's for sure.

Jean Tennent Mitchell

Millennium Wish

Wish time would stand still
Just for a while,
And catch everyone
All the world, with a smile.
Wish time could just change
And life be at peace.
And colour and race
All hate, just cease.
Wish peace and love
Would spread far and wide,
And all we could feel
Was good, deep inside
With happiness for all
What a world it would be.
What a revelation,
All Souls, would be free.

Dorothy Marshall Bowen

Tree Of Life

I will carry into 2000 a heartful of beautiful things
I will nourish and blend all these 'feelings' as I taxi the
runway and take wing
Pausing only too remember pleasures simple and true and embracing
the ache of not having you.
In this life and the next, where no life is in vain
I will stride purposefully onward trying always to smile
through the pain, yes I *will* carry into 2000
All the very precious things, the plans and the promises and an
'appreciation' of all these things,
But, none of us can really do justice to the wonder of the age
Unless we have first 'experienced' the isolation stage.
Long ago will seem just like moments matched in time
And the sneak previews glimpsed back then will finally emerge,
sublime!
I will carry into 2000 hope and spirit to last
I will make it sensationally 'different' and will learn from mistakes
of the past
For I have sampled the pleasures of freedom
I have crossed the star-crossed track
I have witnessed the wonder of new growth
Found the key to all this and all that
Oh, how lucky am I - to have seen the sunrise as it crept magically
forth each morn
To have 'felt' the touch of each tiny human form, held close to my
breast newborn.
'Imagine' *all* of this threatened . . . strive to prevent that
Make this a priority task, for tomorrow is the future and next year
will come all too fast.
No need to run to greet it, stroll with dignity, that is enough
Catch the stars each night as they light your path and remember . . .

Carry the *best* of you *with* you, respect yourself and others and take
the good from the last and leave the bad behind
For in the brave new world of 2000
Let us all try to be much more kind?

Elaine Edgar

Our Special Son

You may not have tomorrow
So let's have fun today.
Let's use each precious moment
To laugh, to love and play.

You may not have tomorrow
your time they say is measured.
So when I kiss your little face
It's something to be treasured.

You may not have tomorrow
But today is all that counts
I sing I laugh and keep you safe
But inside my tension mounts.

What will we do tomorrow
If the angels take you away
How can we give you into his keeping?
When we'll have no one here to play.

You may not have tomorrow
Your life clings like a silken thread
And the strands are very fragile
My heart feels full of dread.

Let's not worry about tomorrow
As curled up you sleep in bed
Blonde curls lie damply
Like a halo around your head.

And when one tomorrow
You are no longer there
We know God entrusted us
With your very special care
The angels will have blessed us
With a special little lad.
Who filled our lives with love and joy
You were the best anyone could have.

You may not have tomorrow
So we made each day count.
Our love surrounds and cocoons you
In an ever increasing amount.

You may not have tomorrow
But your presence will be ever near
And in my empty arms
Your love will help me feel you near.

And when some tomorrow
God takes you in his care
We will be left to ponder
Why life can be so unfair.

Sue Cockayne

A Canopy Of Raindrops

Rainbow, rainbow, I wonder why?
You paint your arch across the sky,
Amber, violet and indigo blue
An artists' palette of every hue.
Just a mirage - iridescent dreams
A canopy of raindrops where the sunlight gleams,
Touching earth thro' cloudy skies
Perhaps that's where the promise lies.
No earthly treasure, no pot of gold
But Heavenly arms to safely hold;
God watches over *You* my friend
From the dawn of creation, to Millennium end.

Jean Mackenzie

Gifts From God

Each morning when I waken,
Through the window of my eyes I see,
An endless stream of gifts from God,
Given to you and me.

Summer sun in the blue, blue sky,
Sparrows flying free,
Butterfly rests gently on the prettiest flower,
Gifts from God for us to see.

Lovers strolling hand in hand,
They stop, they sigh, they kiss,
Baby snuggles in mother's arms,
Surely no greater gift than this.

Love and life, two special gifts,
Given by God who cares,
For each and every one of us,
His special gifts to share.

Brenda Barker

Acceptance

The black silhouettes of trees
Against the orange sky
Golden ripples on the waters
Leaps my heart on high
And even when the dark clouds
Are hanging very near
Although I know their power
Yet still I have no fear.
Likewise the enigma of the hills
Going away to where
Still heedless I go on
And without a care
These gifts of God I understand
For he is there to hold my hand.

Roland Seager

Creation

God's gifts shine thro' his creation
The flowers that come in Spring
Roses shining in the summer sun
The singing birds and dancing butterflies.
Bees humming around woodbine
Little lambs gambolling in green pastures.
The golden corn reaped at harvest time
and the orchard rich with fruit.
Stroll to the river bank and listen to
the sweet music of the water as it
flows o'er the pebbles.
The company and laughter of friends.
All these thing reminds us of the gifts
the Great God has bestowed on us.
It's impossible to study nature without
studying God.

Nora Cotter

Gathering Point

We buried the dearly loved on the everlasting hill,
Co-progenitor of our blood and shell,
Youthful sustainer laid to rest and still.

The lap is finished the baton handed back,
To others who pound the wellworn track,
With newer energies and deeper breath.
But when the race is finally over
(Who knows when!), all who participate
Will take their place, first or late,
On the honoured stand.

Down in the Church the Vicar had said
That our loss, our numbness, our emptiness
Was because we were not fully aware
Of God's greater purpose of worldly care;
Being to our limited area wed.

Well here on the hill you can see around,
The immediate townships lie at your feet,
Movement of cars and people profound,
Gregarious conurbations of houses and streets.
All the anguish, the pain, the cries unheard
At such a distance - as well as the laughter declared.

The sea laps at the foot of the everlasting hill,
The ship sails carrying who knows what it will,
But leaving wood and bone on the quayside.
On and on smaller and smaller with the ebb tide,
Over the horizon it fades away;
Not as Columbus' sailors thought before
But to another world another shore.

It blows often on the everlasting hill,
Strong and so very chill,
But warm at times peaceful and still.
A wind colourless, substanceless,
Yet finding its way into many situations;
The welcoming gust against sail and boom,
Through the nooks and crannies of discomfort,
The stale air changeless room.

To some there is a misty frill
About the everlasting hill,
Only seen by receptive and tinted lens
Behind the shroud what goes on;
Who knows? but scene changers
Work and get no worldly applause,
Actors do their parts and disappear
From the bright and focusing sphere.

Yet their names are cast,
Individually printed on the programme of life;
And without their fleeting presence
There would be no final act.

Whenever it takes place and how it will,
On some spirit charged everlasting hill.

Eric Ashwell

God . . . Glorious God

In times of worries
The feeling of fear
In times of danger
You can't prevent tears.

When there's darkness
There's also light,
You may be crowded,
But no helps in sight.

You feel is weakness
When you want strength.
You try to speak but
You're out of breath.

Your feelings are turmoil
And life's not worth living,
But forgive the people
Who themselves are unforgiving.

There's nothing you
Can lose, and
There's nothing they
Can gain.

No matter how hard
The situation
No matter how much
Pain.

But there's one thing
To remember;
That things will improve
One day;

Meanwhile put your
Faith in God
For he will surely
Answer your prayer.

Rajmin Begum

Freedom

I took for granted a walk in the wood:
So freely given, it felt so good,
When it was carpeted with primroses,
Oxslips and violets for posies.
To lie snugly in tree, or on cool green grass,
And let the world, just simply pass.
To gaze at a sky so very blue.
See blossom on trees, firm and true.
Listen to water tattooing the brook,
Rushing over pebbles and into nook.
Dabbling your feet in the bliss of cool water,
Or swim in a pond, when told not to linger.
Watch moorhens swim quickly amongst rushes.
And newts blending carefully, matching green colours.
Or the exquisite dragonfly gracefully land
On leaf or stalk, with family planned.
When the hours have happily passed one by,
And the sun is sinking low in the sky
Casting long shadows on the valley below,
All tension has left you as homeward you go.
What more could one ask for such retreat,
With this wonderful gift so free at your feet.

Beatrice Newman

Gifts From God

Known or unknown
Far past or beyond our sight
In our small revolution of a universe
Where all is dark or light
We cannot tell where such great light
Shone millenniums away, in gracious gift
We cannot withstay.

In this world much darkened
In man's shadow, gifts all
Sullied and made unnatural in nature's
Way where joy would be
And his unswerving destruction
Never knowing vile horrors from disgrace.

Few knew the life in sunlight forests
Few saw the uproarious waves all full of life
Few know the soft winds full of birds
For now a new world he would make
Forsake innocence and swift devil-play
Fell our living trees and flowers
And poison our thought for beauties too distant.

Or known levelled or killed in fit after fit
Of cruelties. Even for remembrance.
If few saw the gifts of earth we knew it was the life of life
That can no longer take our breath away.
Except perhaps in ending in such shame.
What more can be said or in it read
Than that these were gifts from God.

John Amsden

Snowdrops

They come in the heart of Winter
Those little pearls of cheer
And I wait with buoyant eagerness
Those first flowers of the year
Now 'tis the coldest of the cold time
And in vain I did not wait
A welter of my intrepid friends
Snowdrops cluster near the garden gate.

Barbara Robson

Looking Up

I see majestic clouds roll by,
Like sand-dunes in the dusky sky.
Awesome in their presence
Glorious moving mountains so high.

Exalted by a landscape
Of enchanting, ever-changing shape.
Humbled by the vastness,
Which softly bids my heart's escape.

In an instant I am soaring
The winds of liberty about me roaring.
For one sweet moment of magnificence
Which fires my spirit with adoring.

Joyful that I have been made aware
With extraordinary tender care
To feel, to see and just to 'be'
I clasp my hands in thankful prayer.

I had been looking, yet not seeing
A person, not a human being
Trapped in world embalmed by 'Trivia'
No surprise then, I had felt like fleeing.

By simply looking up, I found
I was elevated from that 'Weighted' ground
And uplifted by the beauty,
Of a love which knows no bounds.

Karen Link

A Gift

Two small bulbs round and neat
Carefully placed in fertile peat
Adorned by a delicate china bowl of blue
Carefully watched with passion new.
A gift from an Aunt
'Sorry, couldn't find a decent plant.'

They sat for weeks in the glint of the sun
Then reward - they had begun
Two delicate shoots come peeping through
Shiny, green growth brand new.
They grew in stature daily
Tall, upright, no means ungainly.

Then at last their flowers burst in view
A wonderful shade of pale blue
Their scent such a delight
Pervades the room from morn to night.
They look just as if they belong
Beauty worthy of a song.

That little bowl appeared so innocent
An explosion of pleasure - two hyacinths.
There are no words to describe
The pleasure that I derive
From the scent and the sight of this gift
The wonder of nature, a tremendous uplift.

Janet Walsh

My Haven

Lupins, delphiniums, colours divine
In this haven that is mine.
I toil, or is it play
As I tend them day-by-day.
The magnolia, now past its best
Still elegant whilst at rest.
Hydrangeas in pink and blue
Each year their blossom they renew.
Upon the fence a rambling rose
Scenting the air as it grows.
A butterfly rests on a leaf
Its colours bright beyond belief.
In this secret place of mine
Where I lose all sense of time.
Slug, snails and creepy-crawlies too
Have potential meals in view.
This mass of colour in every hue
Is surely God's given clue.
Heaven's on earth for us to see
Surrounded by peace and serenity.

Gloria Hargreaves

[1]

By my tears and sorrowing heart
Should He not know.
I cannot see His face or hear His voice
Though longing so.

I am the same yet not the same,
The mirror of my soul
Shows more than does this house of flesh -
I am not whole.

Broken are my dreams and cast away,
With empty hands
I cast about for long-past joys,
Lost in running sands.

The sadness of a love that cannot give -
A cross that I do bear -
This strange companionship to Calvary
Must all men share.

Ah, man made words and God the voice,
They were not fashioned
For desp'rate cries or pleas wrenched forth
So deep impassioned.

The chains of life are the blood in my veins
A tide that flows
And bears my spirit ere I go from hence,
Where, no one knows.

The longing is deep to pass from dark
Into the light.
If only prayer could have the power
To give me sight.

O, come to me in the robes of night
Bright, Evening Star.
And between this world and the next
Place the door ajar.

The vessel of my needs is an empty thing,
All vanities spilt,
And into it with Your loving hands
Put what Thou will.

R L Sharpe

In Loving Memory

Our eyes meeting,
Across the crowded room,
Music, swelling,
Became our favourite tune.

On empty pavements,
Under starry skies,
Our footsteps echoed,
And our arms entwined.

Moonlight gleaming,
Caressing our first kiss.
Young lips touching,
I can recall the bliss.

Oh what promise,
My love, you were the first,
I thought you were my future,
But you became my past.

Barbara Alcock

River Ure

Beautiful, beautiful River Ure,
stretching your legs at Hack Fall, why have
you been hiding your wonderful curves,
your turquoise colours, currents and flow
from me all of these years?
Autumn trees, your leaves before God
will stop hiding from me? All my life
searching - suddenly fully just there!
Spring to eternity.

Robert D Shooter

Wife And Son

Her soft and gentle nature is one to admire,
Her locks are always groomed, as is her whole attire,
Her kindness and her giving is known to all around,
for saying 'No' to anyone, she never has been found.
It's when I'm with this lady, that I'm the proudest man in town,
for no other could match her nature, nor wear her golden crown,
and how I Thank the Lord, for being the luckiest man around.

We first did meet in fifty-six,
at first a wink and then a smile,
this went on for quite a while.
Then one day when twenty-one,
T'was on this day, full of bliss,
I took a chance, one could not miss,
that we embraced for our first kiss.
This confirmed our love of life,
and after dating, named the day,
to become one man and wife.

'Tis without regret she became my wife,
bore a child, a mother of a little life.
Our son he was a little mite,
But Oh, how he put up a fight.
With love and care he won the day,
and how we praise the Lord's display.
Now he's fled the homely nest,
We look at him, he's still the best.
With him and her, I thank the Lord,
for I've been blessed.
He picked them out from all the rest.
So to you both - God Bless.

Derek C J Jones

God The Provider

God is our dear Saviour
He provides for us each day
With food from out the larder
in a sumptuous good array.

He gives to us the flowers
the birds and also bees
The mountains and the rivers
and the blossoms on the trees.

He turns up the sunlight
to brighten all our days
And lightens up the darkness
with the moon's bright shining rays.

The flickering of a million stars
are God's only to be given
So wonderful this mighty scene
that lights the way to Heaven.

So we have a God we trust
on whom we cannot do without
So praise him forever and a day
and never more him doubt.

Lachlan Taylor

Gifts From God

You O Lord gave us the gift of life,
Our heart, our soul, our gift of sight.
The gift of a brain you gave to us,
Filled with thoughts, love and trust.

The gift of life is a wonderful thing.
Up there in Heaven the angels sing
The hymns and praises in good voice;
You gave us all the gift of choice.

These gifts O Lord came from You
To help us all to see life through.
You gave these gifts to one and all
To keep faith with You until You call.

Francis Allen

Spring

Sinks the sun beneath the distant haze
And hurries day towards predestined doom,
Its joyful colours fast submerged in gloom.
The end of days?
So, Winter too appears to play the king
Deceiving prostrate Nature he's the master of the earth
While She prepares in silence and in darkness her rebirth;
Comes on the Spring!
So, with such powerful witnesses before our eyes
As morning every day and Spring's repeated splendour.
How can we fail to grasp God's infinite agenda
And welcome that great Spring when we ourselves shall rise?
Where is Death's sting? O, where indeed,
When buried lies the living seed?

Vaughan Stone

Blessings

I have the sun to shine by day,
To keep me warm and light my way.

And when in bed at night I sleep,
The moon and stars their watch to keep.

I have the showers and summer breeze
The garden crops and leafy trees.

A garden for my leisure hours
In country lanes and wayside flowers.

Amazing creatures small and great;
Far too many to contemplate.

Changing seasons guaranteed,
Food to satisfy my need.

Loving friends their help to give
A comfy home in which to live.

God's creation all around
Wonder, blessings, that abound.

Every day my thanks I give
For the gifts that I receive.

Though a sinner self-confessed
With what wonders I am blessed.

Janet Cavill

God's Triumphant Gifts

What joy good earth brings
The soaring skylark sings.
Woodland creatures revel in their life,
Strong spreading seas that flow,
Clouds above, winds that blow;
Throughout creation God's bliss is rife.

Pure life, skilled work, art,
Blest Spirit you impart;
To serve the common good all our days.
In doubts of age and youth,
We find light in your truth;
Worthwhile tasks, clear vision, shine always.

In trouble, pain, strife,
Your Cross leads to new life.
Beyond all selfish human madness,
Your Providence makes known;
Prevailing hope our own.
Deathless love joins trust, reigns in gladness.

Christ's kingdom has won,
Evil's stronghold is done.
In hostilities He breaks our chains.
Christ is alive, here, now;
Easter strengthens our vow.
No fear of death destroys Christ who reigns.

One triumphant band,
From every urban land;
Vaster than wild hordes with lethal fire.
Great anticipation.
Loud our celebration;
Alleluia Heaven's hosts aspire.

James Leonard Clough

Faith

(To my late wife)

Now, now! Lord Jesus, make me now believe
since you have humbled me and taught me love
that, though I die of grief, I shall not grieve
when I shall see Your face, and my lost dove.
Though Death persuade me mortal life is vain,
and though my darling in my arms lay cold,
yet may I know from your example plain
Death shall release her, and her arms enfold
me once again, body and mind perfected.
Teach me, Lord, in my remaining years
to cleanse myself lest I should be rejected
by so pure a soul and left in tears.
Then, she in Heaven twice lost to me in Hell,
I in this sorrow must forever dwell.

Bernard Brown

Untitled #41

Darkness
Will soon be gone
In a star free sky
The Pale moon mourns

Giving way
To deep reds and golds
In the wake of night
As a day unfolds

The gentle glisten
Of dew kissed grass
In the early hours
That comes to pass.

Pat

God's Gifts To Man

He gave us eyes that we might see
the wonders of his world.
Not only the beauties of his flowers and trees;
not only his living creatures of the seas;
but wonders far beyond the stars.

He gave us ears that we might hear
the music of his universe.
Not only the sound of the birds and the bees;
not only the sound of the wind in the trees;
but sounds deep in the human soul.

He gave us a tongue with which to praise him,
all the days of our lives.
He gave us limbs, not only for our own use,
but so that we could serve him.
Not only for our pleasure, but without measure,
to serve his creatures and those in need.

He gave us of his unstinting love, over and above
that which we deserve.
What can we give him in return? A contrite heart?
Our unworthy selves? Keep faith with his holy word?
He asks so little for his bountiful gifts.
How can we match God's greatest gift to man?
Our Lord and Redeemer,
His only Son.

Fuchsia Coles

A Rose

There is none can compare with the beauty of a rose,
Fragrances so sweet wafting gently up the nose,
Perfectly formed petals open up to form its face,
And to think of its formation,
Fills the heart and mind with Grace.

After all,
They're only atoms
most peculiarly designed,
Just electrons, protons neutrons,
In their own way re-aligned.

But the Masterly approach,
To this majestic work of art,
Indicates the gentle nature
and the sweetness of God's heart,
Love is symbolised,
In its pure and simplest form,
And it reaches its perfection,
In the summer when it's warm.

Dave Sawyer

Gifts From God

In youth I was a dancer and would weave
Patterns and shapes upon the stage,
Partnering the music with balletic skills
Until the time had come to leave.
When I could dance no more
I turned to Pottery.

Taking the clay into my hands
I felt excitement rise. I moulded it
And made it dance upon the wheel
To form new shapes and I could feel
The movement and the rhythm once again.
I used my fingers to enhance
And traced designs as in a dance.

The clay grew heavy, then I felt the urge
To write. Poetry became my medium.
Poems came unbidden to my mind
Became a source of new delight,
When patterns formed themselves in words
And showed themselves upon the page.
These three gifts, if I may call them so,
Have served me from my youth
Into old age.

Christina Stowell

The Sun's Eclipse

The eclipse of the sun, a momentous occasion,
Filling us all with a sense of elation,
One of nature's phenomena, breathtakingly rare.
Which we, as a nation, were able to share.

A pity we couldn't view it with naked eye.
But forewarnings had explained the reason why,
The sight is too precious to risk being impaired,
No matter how much the pleasure we shared.

But television came to the rescue, thousands glued to the screen,
Watching with incredulity the unfolding scene.
The moon slowly blotting out the sun's bright light,
Turning what had been day, into scenes of night.

Automatic street lights came on, aiding everyone to see,
Birds flying to roost, obviously all at sea,
Temperature dropping steeply, a chilly atmosphere,
Making for feelings, spooky, eerie and definitely queer.

Some were fortunate to see the eclipse unclouded
While for others the view was all shrouded,
But whether watched with special aids or television,
It must surely be remembered as a spectacular occasion.

E K Jones

In Gratitude

Thank you fallen Comrades of
World Wars one and two,
For the freedom we now live in,
Which was given to us by you.
Thank you fallen Heroes of
Every race and creed.
Who sacrificed their lives
For the liberty we now receive.
Thank you fallen Saviours,
There's so much more I could say,
But I'll close with God Bless,
And thank you for the life I have today.

Barry D'arcy

Peter Peter!

'How many times have 'you' denied Christ Jesus?'
As did Peter, 'the' first chosen; by the Lord
He denied he knew God's son, yes; he was frightened,
and denied our Saviour Jesus' whom he adored!

Jesus Christ our Lord had solemnly warned him,
that very night that He would be betrayed.
E'er the Cock crowed he'd have denied Him thrice,
Poor Peter did because he was afraid.

And when the Cock did crow, Peter remembered
and in shock realised His Saviour, he had denied,
Now he was alone, desiring to atone; but Jesus was gone, so how
could he repent
In despair and sick at heart, he knew he'd lied.

So, Peter chosen by Jesus to be His number one,
had let Him down, when He was most in need.
This is God the Father's way, to chastise all those He loves.
Yes; first they must be humbled, to succeed!

Fatty R

Voyeur's Scope

The vision was clear, precise and direct, all the stage was set. In readiness.

The couple laboured, trudged and fought their way through the dry and yet arid land. Both tired and weary, yet driven by faith. The earth was hard, unyielding beneath their step, the surroundings inhospitable, thirst and hunger accompanied them as would a shadow. She was with child, very near now was the birth. He was with worry, anxiety etched his brow, fear confused his thought. She never doubted, not for an instant, but then she never had. Hills all around, the conquest of one would only beckon another. Sand in their shoes and at hand.

Finally the arrival upon the small village, too tired to even rejoice. Darkness threatened and with her cold, he must now find shelter. Disappointment everywhere, each crook or cranny, hope now drained from his soul, to be replaced with panic. 'Oh help me that which directed me on this course, pity and comfort if you have any.' He'd failed, was miserable, must beg for her safety, must surely find help, some source of friendship. He must protect her, the burden was his. Yet he'd tried all he could. Such utter despondence. Then almost by chance he asked a singular woman and indeed she knew of a place. His partner showed no surprise or relief, she expected in more ways than one. He led them as told, indeed the placed proved far from grand and the keeper not particular to do business, yet he seemed to soften and showed the way to a lowly place, but warm and somehow holy. They were left alone, and the woman laboured alone, painless, unhurried and free, and the wonder of birth filled the man's eyes.

He comforted her, yet she seemed at rest and the child appeared to acknowledge each movement. Visitors came, it was quite beyond his comprehension, they were all in awe, respectful, at peace, only their blessings did they wish to bestow. He'd ceased to understand, just coped. The babe, though serene, seemed appreciative and smiling, his head though swathed, was caressed in light, the light of love.

At last he found a corner and began to surrender to sleep, yet as he did so the pin of light in the sky caught his eye. It appeared to move. He sighed bewildered, failed to comprehend and gave way to dream.

High above the craft withdrew, the watcher withdrew his gaze, all sense filled with wonder and peace. Then set off anew, so many would sight what was seen through Him.

They moved away from the scene below where each act would follow in turn. A new course was set, now taken, as another journey began.

And it did

L Norbury

Flying Into The Millennium

The sparrows dart and weave their tapestry,
A mystical web of Inspiration it may be,
Beneath the heavens, for you and me
Although God's own winged messengers
Fly, entwined in two's, their secrets to bestow
Not one falls . . . .
Without He knows
Singing and dancing they fly from their awakening dawn,
Into the new millennium morn.
The earth rests, waiting to be restored.
And weapons forged into ploughs and time infinite.
Our hopes to be fulfilled into your everlasting glory.
To wake up and find everything anew.
We go back to perfection and the sweet garden,
And for those that heard and kept God's word
To see the everlasting humming bird.
The enchantment of a new beginning.
Castles of clouds, amidst a rainbow of everlasting light, so true.
Waiting for me and you.
In eternity.
And blossom falls like confetti adorned for the bride and
Oh to be by your side
No more waging of war
No daunting future of lies, and evil gone.
Our minds to heal and we to live on in God's love and Grace,
Embraced,
And to sing the song of the new Jerusalem.

Caroline Frances Ballard

The Search

I'm searching for a garden;
Eden - renewed, again made whole,
Full of natural beauty;
Sweet solace for the soul.

I'm searching for the signpost
Pointing out the way
On and on I stumble;
Mustn't linger; mustn't stray.

I'm searching for the gateway
Inviting me inside;
Desperate to find the place
Where love and peace abide.

I'm searching for the Saviour's hand
To lead and succour me;
To take me from this barren land
And set my spirit free.

I'm searching for the day when
Christ returns to save the earth;
His second coming giving us
New life and hope, new birth.

Margaret M Burke

Now When They Heard Of The Resurrection Of The Dead Some Doubted
(Acts 17:32)

And what shall we say to those who laugh
that God in Man could die?
And then - incredible joke! -
could rise up from the dead?

I think, if we look back,
we just said, 'I believe'.
But oh the dreadful consequence!
It's not a matter of two words.
They place you face to face with Him
and then you can't back down.
You're locked in His regard.
If someone laughs you hardly hear.
You're zero now, and through you
God looks back at Himself.

Inevitable as time
come loss, surrender, death.
For Death is there - a kindly guide -
you know him when he comes.
He gently disengages you
and cuts your mooring chains.
Then light as joy you float out
on the dark deep of God.
For what is death but giving?

In His own Man's life God gave Himself,
taking in Him all the world.
His own God's life received us
to be partakers of Himself.
So when they laugh give them the code.
It's just that matter of two words.
Then they'll share the awful mirth,
cascading through the universe,
of jubilant sons of God.

Jennifer Hashmi

Jesus Lived And Died For Me

Beside the crib on bended knee,
The shepherds gaze and wise men three
A saviour born to set men free
For Jesus lived and died for me.

Beside the lake of Galilee
He spoke of life eternally
A saviour born to set men free
For Jesus lived and died for me.

Upon the cross at Calvary
He said I'll forgive if you follow me
This Saviour
Born to set men free
Now lives again in you and me.

D Sheard

Untitled

I have come to the conclusion
My faith - the Faith
Is not to be fitted in with life!

My faith is the stone cross
Picked up on the wayside
Heavy; a cut-off piece of metal
Hard and cold, - a bit rusty.

The real world,
like those Central American
Street-kids
As orphans
Beaten up; shot
by police, their supposed protectors and stand-in
parents.

I do not know what to make
of others' religious experiences.
Which one to follow;
a heightening of emotion
and then disinterest.
Just like the world
the pleasure, interest, pre-occupations
They do not last.

Yes, it really is not about self,
but others.
Give, and you receive, said Mother Theresa.
That means: you get back your faith.

Do not try to fit in with others, that does not work.
Just the Gospel of Christ and poverty.
That will win every time, and Jesus will lead you -
In the life to come.

H Smith

Save Me

It's Friday again, the dealers arrive.
Cash at the ready, like bees in the hive.
Armani suits and Gucci shoes, nice set of wheels.
Like vultures they swoop, clawing their deals.

Desperate, lost and alone, the hell began to seed.
False friends bring joy, rolled in blissful weed.
Slave to the hash, must have the smoke.
Then steal for gain, to pay for the coke.

The nights do tremble, the days withdrawn
Life lost to despair, from dusk to dawn.
To ease the pain, an injection of gold.
Somebody save me, don't want to be sold.

Cast out of the family, they don't understand.
Disgrace to their door, sent from wonderland.
Escape in my dreams, drowning in sorrow
Please God come save me, make it tomorrow.

Like cancer it grows, craving the drug.
What's it to be then, a man or a mug.
The choice is life, redemption the heavenly bell.
God's mercy be mine, goodbye pits of hell.

Alexander Campbell

Give Me Strength Lord

Today I hung my head in sorrow
I can't keep the tears from my eyes
All my dreams and my hopes have gone forever
So how can I put on paper what I feel in my heart
It's so very hard don't know where to start
There was a beginning - one time in my life
I seem to have lost it just like my wife
She was my strength my anchor in life
She was my friend she was my life
I can't seem to cope with my everyday thoughts
My memories of her just make me distraught
Maybe I should praise the time we both had
But the things we had planned make me so sad
Most of all about the child we never had
Or is it I'm trapped in my lonely fear
Maybe my grief is a sign she is near
I just feel so lost in this life without her
And I'm so hurt within my faith is not strong
But I'll still hope and pray to be with her one day.

Thomas Boyle

A Voice To Sing The Second Time Round

Having lost my singing voice at the age of twenty-four years
After my dear mother died on 'D' Day 1944
More years than I can remember
Have rolled away until eighteen years ago
With the precious love of my Lord God
I once again began to be able to sing.
My heart was elated with great joy
This voice I had been given
Was not at all like my voice in the days of my youth
But far superior, a voice I so much loved
God's special tone of singing voice
I never imagined I could produce
With every heart string I rippled with tremendous volume
Now I sing to the glory of God and his wonderful Son Jesus Christ
Many times I have thanked my very best friends
It is magnificent to sing the second time round!

Alma Montgomery Frank

Prayer For Patience

Father, hear the prayer I pray
Give me patience every day
Teach me how to seek and find
Quiet hope and peace of mind.
Thoughtful in my words and deeds
Understanding others needs
Father, let me always be
Patient, as you are with me.

William Price

A Prayer For Milosevic

Crouching, praying, afraid to move
footsteps, yells and shots.
Soldiers with guns push and shove
What is this evil plot?
Away from home, we're herded now
don't look back at all.
The homes we love are all in flames
our loved ones scream and fall.
The station's there and in the dark
into cattle trucks we're shoved,
the old, the young, and pregnant too
their hands are cruel and gloved.
No air, no peace, the smell of fear
why are we treated thus?
And then outside, we have to walk
we can't take car or bus.
We tramp on through the horrid night
our feet are raw and bleeding.
We have nothing, yes that's true
'it's help that we are needing.
No water, food or even warmth
our babies cry with hunger,
What will we do now, hope is fading
where can we go for succour?
We crouch together, many people
together in our misery.
Soldiers come, but they are kind
for we are part of history,
the shameful kind, remember well
our faces hold the key,
this may happen again one day
to people like you and me.
Yes we have different names and faces
but we are flesh and blood,
my child, he feels pain and fear
just as your child would do.

This baby cries out for his mother
the same as any child.
Look beneath the skin and faith
and see your fellowman,
do not treat him like a dog
be kind, you know you can.
The world is a wondrous place
with plenty for us all.
Stretch out your hand, let your gun fall
break down this evil wall.
Wipe away the mother's tears
and feed the starving child,
Lets be human for a change
not savages from the wild.
These people all deserve to be
left to go their way,
treated fairly and decently
as you would like to be!

Cheryl Mann

Carol

(Possible Tune: Montgomery 'How firm a foundation')
11.11.11.11.

The snow chimes are pealing from heaven to earth;
ring out the old feeling, ring in the new birth.
With dawning decision, look upward and scan
miraculous healing, maid's message and mirth.

Hold not in derision the day it began,
when life was a vision and truth was a Man.
When steeples were stables and colleges caves,
to fools with precision was shown God's own plan.

These things are not fables, forgotten in graves;
for see, midst men's Babels, his Spirit that braves
our world, vainly wheeling, with world-over worth;
it's you he enables and through you he serves.

June Chantry

Untitled

That freckled face deserves a place in the midst of our society
He needs a chance to join the dance to prove he's got variety.
But if that chance was never there to free him from his prison
Now can he tell what's right from wrong, where will he set his
vision.

Who knows what gems are in his mind just longing for the light
But all he knows is blood and blows from seeing *partners* fight.
He has never watched a sunset or a rainbow's crimson hue,
The only animals he ever sees are made at school with glue.

To see him walking on the streets all loud and late at night.
There's no condoning what he does yet that don't make me right.
If he's not taught, he's lost his way for learning makes one free.
Sometime ago someone once said *'You do all this for me'*

A drink of water in my name, a hand when others stare.
The man from Galilee said that his price has paid our fare.
He can only work through people who will follow him each day
To fight the fight and run the race on the Damascus way.

The underdog, the underfed, the poor and underrated
Are joined in with that freckled face, with the face that Jews all hated.
To understand our brother's need and see him in God's grace
It's there but for the will of Him he's standing in my place.

To put him on our donkey and to bathe his wounds with oil.
Then if the need exceeds the cost to go the extra mile
It all sounds so way out to me, to give, to give, to give.
But when we grasp this message I believe we start to live!

Alan Lucas

103

Jesus Of Nazareth

Dear and gentle child, in a manger lay. So we might be saved.
So humble was your birth. Mary knew *you* were special, as
did Joseph too. The angel who visited told them so.

The shining star was the sign for all to follow and to see, such
wonderful silence, so precious was *he*. Everyone wanted to
see this very special baby, bringing so much joy for all the world
to see and to behold.

Wise men came to see *you*, so did shepherds and kings. They
had travelled from near and far, to bring their gifts for *you*.

We would come to know *you* had the greatest gift of all to
give the human race.

We had to wait a while until the child was a man, so much for you
to learn about. First as a carpenter, later as your Father's chosen
one. Who would save all the sinners of this world.

You went to find some fishermen, who would be true to *you*. All were
except one. *You* let him come with you, because *you* knew this was
part of your Father's plan.

You travelled far to cure the sick and the lame. Love and grace
you brought to all. Your healing power shone in every face.

Soon *you* knew *you* would be hung from a cross. This did not
stop *you* from fulfilling your Father's promise. To bring salvation
to our soul. *You* would endure the pain upon the cross.

The treasured child who in a manger lay, would be honoured and
worshipped. *He* would be called *The King Of Kings*. So special was
He to live and die for you and me.

He rose again to give to all the wonderful gift of Eternal Life. *He*
lives still and always will dear *Lord* and saviour of this world.
Who was *Jesus* of Nazareth a dear and gentle child.

Brenda Russell

104

My Only Lord

Stand still and know that I am Lord,
Showers of blessings I will bestow upon you.
My love is greater than He who made me,
I was born to die and live eternally.
At the right hand of my Father on high,
With tears of blessings when I die.
Perfection in everything up in the sky.

Heather Ann Breadnam

Just Be Still

Life brings more than its share of trouble
And often we cry 'Help me Lord'
Then we fight and struggle manfully on
Never heeding his precious word.
We have no time to wait for Him,
To work a miracle in His time.
We feel, perhaps, that we know best
And if we overcome, the glory will all be mine.
'Be still' - my child - The Father says
The problem's already been solved.
'For I know the end from the beginning,
In my time it will all be resolved.
Meanwhile, I say just be still.
As a child in its mother's arms
For haven't I promised - from the beginning of time
To shield you from life's wildest alarms.
So - just be still - - - '

Irene Spencer

The Day The World Stood Still

Many years ago, when the world stood still -
No bell flowers nodding - no wind upon the hill;
Oceans stilled their tides, tempests stayed at bay.
No phenomenon of nature could match this golden day.

The birds and beasts and living things turned in homage to the East.
The world stood by in wonderment, from the highest to the least.
An Infant Child was sent from God to die and save us all.
To suffer at the hands of man in response to God's own call.

How could a new-born child bring such unimagined joy?
How could all be calmed by just a baby boy?
And yet the Christian world each year renews this special day.
There are those who do not believe and yet it never goes away.

There is never any need to doubt - the story stays the same.
The little scene at Bethlehem keeps alight the burning flame.
We believe, we trust, we hope in time to end in Heaven above
Where we will find for evermore the promise of his love.

Ronald Moore

The Wind

Wind crashing against the wall
Flooding down every hall.
Trees fighting to stand up straight.
Wind in a hurry like it can't wait.
The fire burns bright
Day fades into night.
The wind stampeding through every room.
Trees stand to face their final doom.
But the wind is still crashing against the wall.
And last but not least through the great hall.

L M Goodwin (13)

God's Values

Ever-decreasing values
In all the aspects of life -
Is what we are facing
In our daily strife.

A godless tide is sweeping
Through the world as was foretold -
Forecast in the Bible
As wisdom does unfold.

So check the armour that you wear -
See no chinks appear.
The enemy is on the prowl -
But Jesus he does fear.

Stand together Church of God -
United as you pray -
For God is always near to you
And listens to what you say.

As we move to pray to Him
Be humble and contrite.
It is only because of Jesus
We are righteous in God's sight.

Stand up and be counted -
In God's Kingdom be a part -
For His values could be everyone's -
His Son could reign in their heart.

Pat Melbourn

New Ages

A new millennium dawns
The old one has gone.
So many changes
Down through the ages.
Were they for better -
Or worse.
With human intervention
Tampering with nature's plan
Altering lives - and the land.
Making us doubt, and fret,
And yet! hope for the future
Lies deep, in the heart
In the prayer
That the next generation
Will learn the right way
To play their part.
And make the world
The way God meant
It to be from the start.

Catherine McGettigan

Tea For Two

A young boy ran out of school,
and ran, and ran, and ran.
Today he was feeling happy,
he was having tea with gran.

Faster and faster he did run,
this lad could run for hours.
As he rounded a bend in the road,
lots of people, cars, and flowers.

He searched a sea of faces,
and found his mum and dad.
'Mum, why are they wearing black,
and crying, or looking very sad?'

'Gran's having tea with Jesus,'
said mum as tears began to flow.
'Mum would they mind if I went too,
after all it is my turn you know?'

William D Dawson

Patience

Waiting for a train one day
How long the time did seem.
So long to wait
Finally from the distance
She is seen
How beautiful it's finally here.
Patience.

Waiting for a bus to come
On the High Road,
A young boy left the stop
For one further on -
A moment later the bus came
He missed it.
Patience.

The Lord has gone up with a shout,
This same Jesus will return.
Are you thinking of hopping out?
Patience.

Because like the bus and like the train,
Our loving Lord will come again.
He'll take you away
And He'll dry your tears
And you'll live with him for 'a million years'
Patience.

Yvonne Sturge-Prince

Three Gifts For God

Three men there lived who were of goodly age
A labourer, a scholar and a sage,
Who heard God's call as each lay in his bed
Then journeyed to the place where meet the dead.
Each bore a gift for God from his life's toil
A treasure won at cost from muck and moil.
The working-man stepped forward with a crumb;
The other two looked on as if struck dumb.
'Here is a loaf of bread,' said he content,
The others stood there wond'ring what he meant.
The scholar now paced forth in confidence
And showed his gift to God with pride immense.
A jagged piece of glass lay in his hand
All silvered on the back as if 'twere grand.
'Here is a mirror, think on it as you will.
Your eyes may gaze till they have ta'en their fill.'
And all the while God watched with musing eye
Yet was not moved to sound out a reply.
Now 'twas the sage's turn and he moved forth
To visit unto God of his life's worth.
With empty hands unto his Lord he came
Expecting words of condemnation, blame.
God rising, spoke: 'We seek not any rift,
O ancient sage: declare to me your gift.'
'I brought a gift that poured forth heat and light
And helped reveal the path here through the night,
For ' 'twas a candle. Greatly were we anguished
When, far before your throne, it was extinguished.'
God noticed how the sage's thumbs and fingers
Were reddened like a Yuletide carol singer's.
'Of all the gifts, I value yours the most
- your empty hands give *you* no cause to boast.
You gave yourself that others, too, might see;
Step forward into *my* light and know me.'

Rod Treseder

The Compass Of God

Salvation's a complicated concept.
It's not instinctive or natural for man.
It doesn't enter into children's head
nor does it bother a primitive clan.

So how did this weird idea develop
in our psyche? Presupposing a Fall
from Grace? Why did the Creator not slap
down Satan, the evilest fiend of all?

Why was Satan allowed into Eden,
the pasture of Adam and Eve? Surely
he needed ejection from this garden
into hell . . . burning for eternity.

These are pertinent questions. And answers
are totally unsatisfactory.
Religious scenario confers
on the Almighty zero ESP!

Could God not foresee the coming future?
If He could then nothing's original
except what His own divine mind pictures.
Ergo, original sin's nonsensical.

Each day grows a bit more the mind of man
And the Compass of Beliefs holds greater span.

Shafi Ahmed

114

God And The Devil

I rule the Earth, and you have your Heaven,
Said the Devil to God with a leer.
The Universe I made in days of seven,
God answered with a cheer.
You've got it wrong, the Devil replied,
I gave you aid with that task.
Yes, You were there, God gave a sigh,
But you didn't do what I asked.

I went to Earth and did what I could,
While you stayed to set up your Heaven.
The waiting was long, but it felt very good,
My planning took me longer than seven.
You tricked me, God said, while you waited,
For my image to be born on the Earth
I loved you, but you only hated,
And you decided to corrupt my new Birth.

Your claim, God said, has me baffled,
You say you want half of my Birth.
For thousands of years we have battled,
Over my image, that I put on Earth.
Half at the moment is fair, the Devil replied,
But our battle goes on, for Earth is mine.
I am sure to win, might is on my side,
God, you are too sweet, and so divine.

W L Downes

God Has Given Me

God has given me a good life
Nice and simple every day
In the way I breathe and live
It is a simple way.

God has given me a good life
As I look around
Around at all the different things
That make all the sounds.

God has given me a good life
With plenty of peace of mind
But it is the simple things
That he keeps so nice and kind.

Keith L Powell

My Broken Child

Fences hide the run-down scenes
Of broken lives lived in between
A Parent's Partner, Lover, Friend
In tearful loveless lost dead end.

Your Social Worker's here today
Amidst the living shirk and play
You get attention any old way
Legal or not from day to stay.

I saw your saintly smile just once
A kindly thing I said by chance
That spoken junket touched your heart
God Bless you child when we're apart.

Mike Morrison

Land O' The Leal
(*Realm Of The Faithful*)

If you have a perception of yourself
  And in giving of yourself, expect no praise or reward.
    You are ploughing a furrow through immortal earth
Know then, you are sowing seeds for The Almighty Lord.

If your soul, mind and ears are listening,
  To every tiny whimpering sound of pain or fear.
    Should one tear of yours fall in sympathy.
Know then you have irrigated fields of compassion here.

If your heart and eyes see men, beasts and birds,
  Lost and floundering on forgotten untilled land.
    Should you stop and open wide your arms, just once!
Know then you have reaped lost hope by your hand.

If the basis of your prayers to The Father is of love,
  The unification of all people to exercise goodwill.
    Know then, from where you issued and you will return
To the fertile soil of the Land o' the Leal.

Rhys Reese

God's Light

God's light to the earth of ours
Is the light from the sun in the sky?
The world rotates on its own axis
A day and night in twenty-four hours
The seasons of spring, summer, autumn and winter
Are depending on the sun for their coming
In the spring flowers start and birds are humming
And nature is a stir and a good worker
Spring is the time of year when nature awakes
Bringing the flowers and the leaves on the tree
Later, daffodils, Bluebells and later still the Sweet Pea
Winter has lost its frost gone are the white snowflakes
The world goes on in its own orbit around the sun
And at a distance the winter is here
When the sun is closer to the world, summer is near
The world goes around the sun in a year, what fun
In the summer time it is hotter and the days are longer
The flowers are at their best when they adorn any place
Roses in colour and a pansy with its pretty face
The fragrance fills the place with wonder
The autumn again strips the trees of their leaf
After trees that bear nuts have dropped them
Hazelnuts with very hard shells roll up your sleeves
And to gather them you have to bend
When winter comes again we soon begin to feel the cold
The young ones are all right but it's different if were old
The frost, snow sleet and icy condition will end

R T Owen
  A Beaumaris Lad

God's Promise

The bow that arches the sky
After the storm has abated
Such beauty for all to see
The wonder that God created.

A rainbow with lovely colours
Reminding us of God's covenant
To all people here on earth
From which He would never recant

The promise God made to Noah
That all flesh would not be destroyed
By the flooding of the waters
Which he (God) would always avoid.

Who can say there is no God
When there's so much proof around
The sea, the sky, the heavens above
God's love and goodness that doth abound.

Ref:- Genesis Chap. 9 verses 8 to 17.

Dorothy Price

God Of Many Places

Loving God, Holy God,
You are there in the strong church tower,
A place offering security
Against attack by the evil one.

Loving God, Holy God,
You are there in the quiet stillness,
A place offering peace
Amidst the world's noise and bustle.

Loving God, Holy God,
You are there in the candle flame,
A place offering light
And dispelling the darkness which threatens.

Loving God, Holy God,
You are there in the sycamore seed,
A place offering new life
After the death of the spring blossom.

Loving God, Holy God,
You are there in the heart of every follower,
A place offering warmth and love
To those suffering cold and rejection.

Loving God, Holy God,
You are there in so many places
Around the world you created,
Waiting to be found by those who seek you.

Paul W Fleming

Forgiven And Loved

Tired and weary I sank to the ground,
All around me there wasn't a sound,
With head bowed I gazed at the floor,
Ashamed because I'd failed Him once more,
Then Jesus' voice so tender with love,
Filled my heart with peace from above,
His strong loving arms helped me from the ground,
Dusted me down and turned me around,
'This is the way, now come follow me,
And the way ahead I'll help you to see,'
Forgiven and loved I set out anew,
Determined to accomplish what I'm called to do,
To Jesus we're special and He loves you and I,
Whenever we stumble He's standing by,
To comfort and strengthen and show us the way,
Guiding us safely through each passing day.

Amanda Monger

Lonely . . . Not Alone

Lord I love you

But I feel so alone

Lord I love you

I can't make it on my own

Lord I love you

Show me what to do

Lord I love you

Help me, pull me through

Zarine Billam

For He Loves Us The Most

Praise to you, my God; my light
For guiding my way so that it's right.
You lift up my shoulders, oh king above kings;
Enfolding my heart with joyful wings.

You are like a shaft of brilliant light -
Filtering through Life's dark dreary night.
Your forgiveness comes through your blessed Son:
Forgiving my sins; He has paid for what wrongs I've done.

With a Golden band, you ease my dread
Of the Grave; for you and I are wed.
I am the bride; you are the bridegroom -
Death can no longer bring darkest doom.

Oh make my soul on you recline,
And on sleep at night; make my eyes gladly dine.
Help me to sleep; so that when I awake -
I may serve you better; for Christ's holy sake.

Is sleep like death, what is it to die?
Now I am saved; I no longer cry -
For shafts of sunlight fill my dreams;
No evil power awakens me with screams.

Praise the Lord, Let his blessings flow,
Praise God, Goodness reaches us below.
Praise Our Father, Son and Holy Ghost;
Praise him always; for He loves us the most.

Sheryl Williamson

Reassuring Seasons

For us who live in Europe's temperate zones
The changing seasons are a wondrous gift
Whose beauties and suggestive overtones
Will give our hearts a never-failing lift.

From Spring's fresh burgeonings and cheerful flowers
Renewing youthful energies and hope
To Summer's showy blooms and dreamy hours,
Earth offers for our comfort endless scope.

Then Autumn burnishes its armoury
To send us forth with courage to the cold,
While, faced by frost and snow's gendarmerie,
Plants sleep at last beneath their wintry hold.

These varied beauties soothe and feed our souls
While symbolism acts upon our minds,
Elucidating our contrasting roles
As through life's changes our own pathway winds.

And when we see the regular return
Of seasons in their sequence every year,.
The hand of our Creator we discern
Maintaining all in order in our sphere.

So alternating death and then rebirth
Serves to increase our faith in God's good care:
He Who so well designed our radiant Earth
Has made a heaven, too, for us to share.

Anne Sanderson

The Lovely Eventide

I Thank you Lord, for this blest space -
Four walls, a roof by storms defaced,
Breaks open to the sky; a place
Of nesting birds in vibrant song.

This Clematis of former days,
Which other hands have loved to tend,
Is clinging yet to crumbling bays
As I to my Arcadia cleave.

The yew trees tap the Hinder pane,
Scant moles and martens comb the brake,
Ringousels swoop to forage grain -
There are no empty hours to grieve.

The delph has gone from Ingles shade
And threadbare wears the tabouret;
Though tapestries that life has frayed
Have deeper tone and firmer woof.

Uncrowded hours full time has wrought
To crown, subtly, these fading years;
For all this eventide has brought
Rise vespers of an ageing heart

Margret Phillips

Precious Things

You can keep your wealth and power
I would give it all away
For the prize of a healthy body
As I travel along life's highway.

You can keep your wealth and power
God gave us more precious things
Like the family that stays together
And the pleasure a close friendship brings.

You can keep your wealth and power
Though you think it is life's magic pill
But it gives not a shred of comfort
When a loved one is terminally ill.

You may think that your wealth and power
Makes you welcome wherever you trod
But of one thing you can be certain
It's no use in the Kingdom of God.

Patrick Greaves

Heavenly Flower

I have seen the heavenly flowers
In all their pinks and green.
I have seen their colours
And some that's in between
I have seen the rainbow river
And seen the purple tree
And now in thanking Jesus
On my bended knee.

I have seen the heavenly flowers
All neatly in a row
I have smelt their pretty perfume
And seen God's angelic glow
I have seen the rainbow river
And seen angels in their youth
And now thanks to my God
I know the truth.

Colin Allsop

Our World

Gifts are a gift from the Creator,
Let us not waste them
Or abuse them . . .

but use them
To make Our World even better.

Jenefer Adams

I Think

I think of those who cannot see,
I think of those who're deaf,
And also those who cannot speak,
And those born with a cleft.

Of those who spend life in a chair,
And those who live with deep despair.
And those with limbs deformed at birth,
And those with different minds from us.

They all have something common to share,
They have love and friendship, one can't compare,
They are loyal, happy and truthful too,
They are really just people like me and you.

Anne J Bourner-Alderman

God's Gift

I am the Gift and I am the Giver.
My bounty flows forth like a pure
timeless river.
Here, limpid my waters, so peaceful and
fair.
Here, radiant, exultant, star-studding
the air.

Come bring your reflections
I'll touch with my light
Till void of defections
all failings come right.
How constant my flowing,
How mighty my arm!
How deep is my knowing!
How refreshing my calm!

How soothing my murmur
to banish all fears!
How rippling my laughter
to wash away tears!
Come, walk by my waters,
Come listen to me.
I'm the Gift, I'm the Giver,
Come, share all with me.

Peter Foster

The Gift Of Communication

My gratitude Lord for pen and ink
My imagination and the sense to think
For Shakespeare's birth we are in your debt
Also, the sumerians and their alphabet
The sonnets of Elizabeth Barrett Browning
Stevie Smith's lines of a lonely man drowning
Every human emotion I can read on a page
Each spoken nuance I hear acted onstage
A gift to use, a joy to create
You gave us the power to communicate.

Jeanette Latta

Cats Everywhere

There's cats on the window sills
There's cats at the door
And cats on the chairs
And cats on the stairs

There's cats on the bed
And also cats on the floors
The cats outside
Are playing on the lawn

There's a cat in a box
There's a cat on the tele
Lying on its belly
And its looks so silly

So how many more cats
Do you think I'll find
Up and down around our town
Well my guess is leave it up to them

Margaret Vale